Listening to God's Voice

Listening to God's Voice

HOW TO HAVE AN INTIMATE, PERSONAL RELATIONSHIP WITH GOD

Marcos Borges

ISBN: 0997341807
ISBN 13: 9780997341805
Library of Congress Control Number: 2016903233
Marcos Borges, Seattle, WA

CHAPTER 1

God Speaks Your Language

You will call upon Me, and you will come and
pray to Me, and I will hear and heed you.

JEREMIAH 29:12 (AMPLIFIED BIBLE)

HAVING A PERSONAL, INTIMATE RELATIONSHIP with God
sounds a lot harder to achieve than it should be in reality. We spend most of our spiritual lives trying to understand our life circumstances and feelings and trying
to determine how we should act and react to all this
events. Having clear communication with God will
certainly make all of that easier.

To me, this always felt like a very delicate process,
since it seemed that the "quality" of my communication

with God was directly impacted by my feelings. I could be having a good day, feeling grateful, and feeling God's love when suddenly something simple—like a problem at work or an argument with a family member—would change my mood, and I simply wouldn't feel as connected to God anymore.

In the early days of my walk with God, this was possibly the most frustrating issue I encountered. I believe that everyone is born with a sense that there is something greater than him or her, and I personally had a very real desire to be close to God, to talk to God, and to understand what or who He was. The feeling was so real, but I didn't know what to do about it! Where can you find God sitting and ready for a visit? What is God's phone number?

I decided that the Bible was the way to go and that I was going to read the whole book. This almost ended tragically because the Bible is not always an easy book to digest. But I began to read it, and very early on, in Genesis 15, I read the story about how God talks directly to Abram and promises him a son and countless descendants. The simplified version of the story is this: Abram asks for a confirmation from God that His promise was real, so God instructs Abram to bring Him a series of animals—a heifer, a female goat, a ram, a turtledove, and a young pigeon. Abram kills the animals and cuts them in two, placing each half across from the other and creating a sort of hallway. Abram goes to sleep nearby and has a nightmare, which God then interprets for Abram. The sun goes down, and Abram wakes up and sees a flaming torch passing between the pieces of animal. What was all this about?

When I first read this story, it increased my frustration and left me with more questions than answers. I was searching for clues about having a relationship with God, and I was getting the impression that communicating with Him required all sorts of rituals, dreams, and animal sacrifices! It was discouraging, and it felt way too complicated. Determined to find an explanation, I researched the story and found that the "cutting covenants," which is the term for the cutting of the animals, was used widely in those days, especially in lands influenced by the Hittites. In a "cutting covenant," two parties would make a pact and swear an oath that they would lose their own lives—just like the animals did—if they failed to keep the promise.

Understanding the background of the story changed my perspective on God. When Abram wanted a confirmation, God responded in a very loving way. He spoke to Abram in Abram's own language. It's likely that these types of ceremonies and covenants were a common sight in Abram's life, and it is possible that he had performed this kind of pact before. God could have just told him to "wait and see" if the promise would be fulfilled, but instead, God had the patience and love to talk in a way that would make sense to Abram.

This is the first key to understanding your communication with God. Think about this: God is not only powerful but also the holder of all knowledge and wisdom. Is a God with all this knowledge incapable of talking to you in a way that you can interpret? Of course not!

In His wisdom, God is more than capable of talking to you on your level and in a way that will make sense to you—just as He did with Abram. A wise God wasn't going to create flawed beings who could not talk with Him. In fact, we're designed with all of the tools necessary to have a relationship with God. We are equipped not only with our physical senses, our brain, and our common sense but also with spiritual ears, a spiritual mind, instincts (gut feelings), emotions, feelings, the voice of our consciences, and a relationship with the Holy Spirit. So you can do it!

You are designed perfectly and with free access to unconditional love and understanding from God. The form of communication that you choose to use with God should feel natural, like a conversation with a friend. Keep in mind that God manifests to everyone in a personal way, as He did with Abram. He is one God, and yet He is an individual God for each person. Don't get confused or frustrated if you communicate with Him differently than someone else at your church or in your home.

If you are part of a spiritual community, this can become confusing. You may hear from other members that God talked to them in their dreams. Other people hear clear, loud voices in their heads. Still others will describe a feeling they had in their hearts. If you compare yourself to them, you might feel discouraged. You might think this: "Maybe I can't hear from God. Maybe God isn't talking to me because He is angry at me." Or you may second-guess yourself, doubting the message that you received in your heart because it didn't come in the form of a dream or a voice.

God has an individual plan for your life and wants to have an intimate, personal relationship with you. And even though everyone perceives God in different ways and hears from Him in different ways, it all comes from the same God, who is the source of all love.

God will make sure to talk to you in a way that you understand, which also means that you are free to ask Him to talk to you in different ways. For example, I didn't really enjoy having dreams because it was difficult for me to fall asleep, so I simply asked God to use other forms of communication with me. Don't be afraid to ask God to talk to you through a voice, a feeling in your heart, a text in the Bible, or any other intimate way that resonates with you. The most important thing is that you keep asking Him. Work at it, and don't give up.

Communication with God will feel like an exercise at the beginning, but it will become easier and clearer over time. Most people are not familiar with talking with God on a regular basis and may have learned to ignore their gut instincts or consciences. So at first it may feel like you're not hearing or sensing anything. But make no mistake: God does answer. Also, keep in mind that people commonly go against what God has told them. People also go against their gut feelings or the voices of their consciences in many areas of their lives—sometimes for very long periods of time. Consequently, communication with God might feel unnatural to you at first. As you ask Him for more intimate communication, you will be reconnected, and the path will become easier.

When Jesus was teaching this principle to His disciples in Matthew 7:7, He told the disciples this: *"Keep on asking and it will be given you; keep on seeking and you will find; keep on knocking and [the door] will be opened to you. For everyone who keeps on asking receives; and he who keeps on seeking finds; and to him who keeps on knocking, [the door] will be opened"* (Amplified Bible).

Notice how the phrase *keep on* is repeated six times, implying an effort on our part to *continue* asking, seeking, and knocking. However, don't let this discourage you. Remember the first key: God is loving, all powerful, and infinitely wise, and He is capable of talking to you every day and in your own language.

The second key is to understand that you are capable of hearing God just as you are. Acceptance and self-esteem are an important part of this second key. There are many reasons that you might feel unworthy of having a relationship with God, and I will cover these reasons in the following chapters. You might feel that you have made too many mistakes, that you have gotten yourself into situations you shouldn't have, or that you haven't been seeking a relationship with God as much as your conscience was asking you to. Even if all of these things were true, God doesn't put conditions or restrictions on having a relationship with Him. All He asks is that you want a relationship with Him and that you ask for it. Due to the infinite love that God has for you, your relationship with God is acquired through grace, due to the infinite love that God has for you. Denying divine guidance may complicate your life and make it harder for you to feel God's presence, but it would never make it impossible for you to talk to God, nor would it never prevent God from talking to you.

You can have an intimate relationship with God in your life, no matter what your current circumstances are, no matter how you feel about yourself, and no matter what good or bad decisions you have made.

If you feel unworthy, it doesn't mean that God won't listen to you, but the feeling of being unworthy may be preventing you from praying as often as you should. Many people choose to be alone and avoid talking to anyone when they're not feeling well. Sadness or the feeling of being unworthy may cause you to have the same reaction toward God. Some days, you won't feel like talking to Him, but God's love is bigger than any other love. It isn't changed by your personal feelings. No matter how terrible you feel that you've behaved, do not stop your communication with God. Allow Him to be your guide and comforter as you straighten your path.

You need to have a real understanding of how perfect God's love is. If you continue to feel unworthy and think that God is angry with you or doesn't love you, you will second-guess any communication from Him, wrongly thinking that He is angry with you. God may be angry with some of the decisions you have made, but He is never angry with you. God gets angry because He understands that wrong decisions will bring negative outcomes in your life, and He would much rather see you happy. In other words, God's anger is *for you* and not *against you*. Regardless of what you do, God loves you and is ready to work for you and with you to bring peace, joy, and deliverance into your life.

Jeremiah 29:11 says, "For I know the thoughts and plans that I have for you, says the Lord, thoughts and plans for welfare and peace and not for evil, to give you hope in your final outcome."

Never diminish the importance of following God's guidance. Faith is rewarding because God in His love and wisdom knows which is the easiest path for you to follow, and He has a multitude of blessings in store for you. In Jeremiah 29, God says that He has thoughts and plans for your welfare, prosperity, and peace, and He exhorts you to have hope for the future. Even if you step aside from His path and suffer a setback in your life, you won't suffer a setback in God's love for you. It doesn't matter what you do—God will always love you unconditionally.

The Bible says to seek the kingdom of God, and then everything else will be added unto you (Matt. 6:33). Don't make the mistake of waiting to change little things in your life—such as going back to church, leaving that bad relationship, or whatever is making you feel guilty and unworthy. Don't try to handle it by yourself; instead, seek God repeatedly. As Jesus said, you should "keep on, keep on, and keep on" talking to God. You should let Him bring you divine deliverance and blessed breakthroughs.

Holding on to unworthiness will only hinder your ability to talk to God. Don't wait to change your life circumstances—ask God today.

reparing errors made with you family, yours children, your ex partners

CHAPTER 2

Expressing Your Emotions

O Lord, you have searched me [thoroughly] and
have known me. You know my downsitting
and my uprising; You understand my
thought afar off. You sift and search out
my path and my lying down, and You are
acquainted with all my ways. For there is not
a word in my tongue [still unuttered], but,
behold, O Lord, You know it altogether.

PSALMS 139: 1-4 (AMPLIFIED BIBLE)

MANY YEARS AGO, I WAS praying fervently to God to bring me deliverance in one area of my life. Over ten years had passed, and I still had not received my breakthrough. One day, I felt that I had waited long enough, and I was convinced that God was just not listening to me. I became filled with anger, pain, and resentment, and I went to the backyard and screamed at God. I said, "You are a joke! You don't take care of anyone. You don't listen to me. You are just torturing me and making me wait!" I went on for quite a while in my rage, even using curse words! After I let it all out, I immediately felt a deep fear about what I had done. "This is it," I said to myself. "God will punish me and won't give me what I was asking for." I remember being invaded by feelings of abandonment, despair, regret, and shame. Just as I was panicking, I heard God's voice saying, "I have been raising kids for hundreds of years. Don't you think I can handle a little fit and continue to love you? Just talk to me."

Telling God how I felt and sharing my frustrations was healing in many ways. It calmed me. It is the same feeling of relief that you get when you are frustrated or sad about something, and a loved one comes to listen to you. We all feel better after hugging a person that we love and crying on his or her shoulder.

This experience taught me that my frustration was only a moment in time. It is not always easy to pursue the right thing in your life. There are many other paths and temptations to follow, and the longer you wait, the harder it may be for you to hold your ground. But as you speak freely to God about your frustration, you allow God to become your comforter.

Jesus taught the disciples that the comforter, who is the Holy Spirit, would always be available for His followers, but I had the idea that I couldn't really complain or say anything negative. So I started wondering this: How can I be comforted if I am not telling God how I feel?

When you are seeking a relationship with God, it is only natural to join churches, religious denominations, or spiritual groups—at least, I know that I did those things. When you are part of any of these organizations, you are taught a lot of information that can be difficult to filter. You're taught about commandments and rules—many of which come from the Old Testament. Although the Old Testament is full of great wisdom, it can also be very confusing and end up obstructing the type of relationship you are entitled to have with God through grace.

Teachings at church can also give you a great understanding of God's holiness, His true and unconditional love, and the power that comes from allowing God to govern your life. You learn to have a grateful attitude, follow God's guidance, refrain from judgment, and have faith. But even though these are all very powerful principles, many people alienate their own feelings in an honest attempt to follow these principles. In some cases, they may feel that they are about to be punished because they weren't grateful or didn't have enough faith. But having negative emotions is not a sin. Yes, gratitude and faith bring tremendous power into your life, but you are still human. Frustration, doubt, anger, and all of your feelings are a part of who you are, and as you learn to control your emotions, you still have to let God help you manage them. This is especially true early on in your relationship with God, which is when you are just beginning to get a handle on your emotions.

I discovered that my problem was that I interpreted all these teachings as commands, so complaining or feeling bad felt like sinning to me. I was living in fear instead of letting God comfort me. Strive to study the scriptures in your private life, not just in church, and pray for revelation and clarification. Doing these things is a great way to learn to hear God's voice. As I did some deeper personal study, I found that the problem with my emotions was not that I felt them—I knew I was free to share my emotions with God. The problem was in the way I acted based on my emotions.

When you act based on your emotional impulses, you will get yourself into messy situations, but you shouldn't condemn yourself for feeling what you feel. Instead, bring all of your feelings into the privacy of your prayers, and enjoy God's love, empathy, and support.

Let's use Elijah's life as an example: "There he [Elijah] came to a cave and lodged in it; and behold, the word of the Lord came to him, and He said to him, 'What are you doing here, Elijah?' He replied, 'I have been very jealous for the Lord God of hosts; for the Israelites have forsaken Your covenant, thrown down Your altars, and killed Your prophets with the sword. And I, I only, am left; and they seek my life, to take it away'" (1 Kings 19:9–10).

Elijah was a powerful prophet, and he lived in a time when the people of Israel were incredibly rebellious against God. They had forsaken all of God's teachings and had begun to praise idols. Elijah was so angry with the whole situation. He felt jealous and saddened for God. So he chose to go hide in a cave. On top of this, he was afraid of losing his life! He had had enough. If you read the story all the way to verse 14, you see that Elijah was so upset that God had to come twice to ask him this: "What are you doing here?" Elijah was completely

15

honest with God both times and said that he was angry, jealous, and afraid of getting killed. God heard Elijah, gave him time, and remained with him, and God didn't even get upset that he had to repeat himself! God heard Elijah's pain and then proceeded to guide him. God operates in truth, which is why being honest with God is so powerful.

While sharing your feelings with God, He might choose to console you or tell you the reason that you're going through a certain situation. He might ask you to do something, or He might request that you keep waiting, keep believing, and keep trusting that He is in control. Regardless of His answer, trying to hold your emotions inside will not do you any good. You may have good intentions to remain faithful, but from time to time, it is all right to say "I don't think I can do this anymore" in your intimate, personal prayers.

This doesn't mean that you should give free license to your emotions and allow them to rule your life. There is a huge difference between sharing your feelings with God in a private conversation and complaining out loud, allowing your resentment or impatience to rule your life and disrupt the peace *or disrupt your own peace*

of those around you. God does not get shocked, nor does He panic at your negative feelings. Instead, you can expect God to be there to hear you, support you, and guide you.

Psalm 145:8 says, "The Lord is gracious and full of compassion, slow to anger and abounding in mercy and loving-kindness."

Once you start a relationship with God, you begin a growth process that moves at different speeds for different people. It doesn't matter how fast or slow your growth is. All that matters is that you are still moving. And God is patient with all of us.

While you are in the learning process, you have free access to God's patience. The Bible repeatedly teaches that God is long-suffering, patient, and slow to anger. You should not be a person who makes all of his or her decisions in the heat of the moment, but if you fail to keep your emotions under control from time to time, don't be hard on yourself. You might need to ask for forgiveness if you hurt someone. You must also have perspective and remember that your feelings were given to you by God to navigate life and that there is nothing wrong with them.

Your feelings will not always bring negative outcomes. In fact, many times God may choose to talk to you through your feelings, which are a part of your common sense. Perhaps there is a relationship that constantly causes you only sadness: God might be talking to you and using those feelings. Request God's confirmation that your feelings are an indication of something more.

You have access to a loving God. God can help you understand why you feel the way you feel and can help you turn your sadness into joy. In the garden of Gethsemane, before He was going to be crucified, Jesus asked God for His burden to be taken away. God still required Jesus to sacrifice Himself, but Jesus wasn't embarrassed to ask for deliverance. God sent Him comforters, and Jesus was obedient because He knew and trusted that God had a reason for His pain. Talk to God about how you are feeling, and use your emotions to your benefit. Be in control of your emotions, not the other way around! Don't let your emotions make you live in fear, angst, concern, or depression. resentment, judgment

Being aware of your feelings when you are talking to God creates powerful prayers. However, this doesn't mean that you will always get what you want. Hebrews 12 teaches that the Lord corrects and disciplines everyone whom He loves. Though it might not prevent your hardship, walking through any situation holding hands with God makes a difference. It is no different with our own children. If a child wants to go play with a ball next to a busy road, and you don't let him or her, your decision will not change just because he or she shares with you how frustrated and confused he or she feels about it. But sharing these feelings allows the parent to lovingly explain why it is dangerous and not the right thing to do. Ultimately, our children must trust that we know better and that we love them.

In the Bible, we learn many things about God's nature, including the fact that He commonly reveals Himself as a father who is far more perfect than any father on earth. Isaiah 49:15 teaches that it is more likely that a woman would forget her nursing child than that God would forget about you.

Isaiah 49:15 says, "Can a woman forget her nursing child, that she should not have compassion on the son of her womb? Yes, they may forget, yet I will not forget you."

Jesus explained this principle with this beautiful example: "What father among you, if his son asks for a loaf of bread, will give him a stone; or if he asks for a fish, will instead of a fish give him a serpent? Or if he asks for an egg, will give him a scorpion? If you then, evil as you are, know how to give good gifts [gifts that are to their advantage] to your children, how much more will your heavenly Father give to those who ask and continue to ask Him! [Even the Holy Spirit]" (Luke 11:11–13).

Embrace the love and wisdom of God, and rest in His arms, trusting that He creates a safe space for you to share how you feel. Expect to be heard and loved. You are free to talk to God. Allow Him to comfort you and guide you.

CHAPTER 3

You Can Speak God's Language

§

Let us love one another, for love is (springs)
from God; and he who loves [his fellowmen]
is begotten (born) of God and is coming
[progressively] to know and understand
God [to perceive and recognize and get a
better and a clearer knowledge of Him].
He who does not love has not become
acquainted with God, for God is love.

1 JOHN 4:7– 8 (AMPLIFIED BIBLE)

GOD IS THE SOURCE OF all love and not just any type of love. He is the source of truly unconditional, perfect love that you receive for free. This means that you get to love yourself just as you are—with your talents and defects! This is good news!

Since God is the source of all love, and since you have learned that God speaks your language, it's now only fair that you learn to speak God's language. How exciting!

Love is God's language. If you don't let God love you, and if you don't love yourself and give love to others, God could be talking to you right now, and you wouldn't know His voice. To know love is to know God, and to give love is to speak God's language.

The Bible teaches that the person who gives love is *"coming [progressively] to know and understand God [and to perceive, recognize, and get a better and clearer knowledge of Him]."* God is love! He will never withhold His love. It doesn't matter what you do, it doesn't matter what you say, it doesn't matter how many mistakes you make, and it doesn't matter how many times you go to church. God has always loved you and always will love you. But you also need to love yourself. How can you give love to others if you don't even like yourself? If you don't love yourself or let God love you, how can you fight the thoughts of unworthiness and self-pity that become obstacles in your relationship with God?

Love is the purest and biggest manifestation of God's power. Love can make you smile and feel comforted, safe, creative, happy, heard, important, and special. Everyone wants to feel loved, and in many cases, people look desperately for love from another person. They live frustrated, angry, or resentful lives because they do not get love in the form they want or from whom they want love from. But instead of looking to get love from someone else, remember that you are privileged to receive love from God and that you can love yourself.

Jeremiah 17:5 says, *"Cursed [with great evil] is the strong man who trusts in and relies on frail man, making weak [human] flesh his arm."* This doesn't mean that it is wrong to receive love from your spouse, children, friends, and family, but if your self-worth and self-love depend on how people are treating you, you are bound or "cursed" to be hurt and disappointed. And isn't it unfair to set such high expectations of your loved ones? They are human just like you are and are moody, imperfect, and full of flaws. It is truly a curse then—not because God gets angry and curses you but because you will become cursed with disappointment sooner or later. If you are putting your personal happiness in the hands of another human, you are being reckless, because he or she is as flawed as you are.

God is not waiting for you to perform perfectly. In fact, God already knows when and how you are going to mess up. Regardless of how you feel or what you do, as you love yourself and God more, you should allow your communication with God to flow more easily.

Many believers struggle with judging themselves. We all hear that voice in our heads that says, "God is not listening to you," or "God is angry at the way you reacted today." Here is how you should respond to those voices: "So what?" God loves you, and He does not condemn you. God is there to help you and give you the grace and the opportunity to apologize if necessary. He educates you with love and shows you how you could have handled the situation better. He will console you.

Self-love and knowledge of God's love are both wonderful and powerful places to be, but you have to work at getting to those places. You don't have to earn God's love, but you do have to work to make it a habit to love yourself and God. If you are having a rough time, it is often hard to have perspective and remember this. It is easy to get discouraged and go back to blaming yourself, others, or your circumstances for your unhappiness and low self-esteem.

So what is the best solution to this? First, remind yourself that you are in right standing with God through grace, so no matter what you do, you can always go straight to the throne of God and receive love, compassion, and help. You don't need any intermediaries—such as rituals, visions, quests, spiritual journeys, hallucinogenic drugs, or anything else. You are capable of starting a conversation with God right where you are—at home, at work, driving, or in the bathroom. The second part of the solution to this problem is to walk in love in your daily life. Practicing the fruits of the Holy Spirit every day will not only benefit your life and those around you but will also enhance your communication with God. Try to remember what the Bible says in 1 John—walking in love gives you a greater understanding of who God is, and you will learn to speak God's language.

The best way to let love operate in your life is to understand the fruits of the Holy Spirit.

THE FRUITS OF THE SPIRIT

> *But the fruit of the [Holy] Spirit [the work which His presence within accomplishes] is love, joy (gladness), peace, patience (an even temper, forbearance), kindness, goodness*

*(benevolence), faithfulness, Gentleness
(meekness, humility), self-control (self-
restraint, continence). Against such things
there is no law [that can bring a charge].*

GALATIANS 5:22–23 (AMPLIFIED BIBLE)

LOVE

*And so faith, hope, love abide [faith—
conviction and belief respecting man's relation
to God and divine things; hope—joyful and
confident expectation of eternal salvation;
love—true affection for God and man,
growing out of God's love for and in us],
these three; but the greatest of these is love*

I CORINTHIANS 13: 13 (AMPLIFIED BIBLE)

Love is the foundation of all of the fruits of the Holy
Spirit. If you love yourself, love God, and love the
world, you will not only harvest great blessings, but
you will also deepen your relationship with God.

When Jesus was asked which was the most important, or the weightiest, commandment, He replied that it was to love God and love others as you love yourself. It's as simple as that.

Giving love creates a happier, healthier, and more stable environment around you. If you are walking around your home feeling miserable, snapping at your family, feeling angry at your friends, or angry about your job, you are not creating a very nice atmosphere. Giving love allows you to create peace around you.

You must persist in this matter. You might try it for a couple of days and feel that there is no change around you. If you are normally a moody person, the people around you might be so on edge that they might not notice a change. Remember that you are not giving love to see what you get from it. You must give love and persist in it, since love can change any circumstance. When you give love, you allow God's power to flow through you.

I believe that most people have become insensitive to the real power of love—maybe because of the way the word *love* is used. A person might say things like "I *love* this TV show" or "I *love* wine" or "I *love* my car." A person can go from saying "I love you" to friends and family to saying "I hate you" after any discord arises. Even at church, a person might say, "I love you, brother," or "I love you, sister," to someone that he or she has seen twice in his or her life! People are either not interested in love or, even worse, think they already understand it completely.

Love is so deep that I don't think we could ever stop learning about it. Do you regularly study what love is? Are you moody when you give love? Are you stable in the way you give love? Real love is healing, powerful, and unconditional. Some people give conditional love in relationships. A relationship or friendship may be great, but the minute that a person's partner does something that person doesn't like, he or she is ready to end the relationship. Indeed, one of the most powerful scriptures about love is 1 Corinthians 13:4–8, and it is quoted in weddings all over the world. We hear it all the time without really meditating on it. Perhaps if more couples took the time to really understand it, fewer marriages would end in divorce or in unhappy circumstances.

You should study 1 Corinthians 13:4–8 over and over and consider researching each of the words to see what the passage really means.

Incorrect translation
"we all have been exposed to this text even if we are not avid Bible readers

Love endures long and is patient and kind;
love never is envious nor boils over with
jealousy, is not boastful or vainglorious,
does not display itself haughtily. It is not
conceited (arrogant and inflated with pride);
it is not rude (unmannerly) and does not
act unbecomingly. Love (God's love in
us) does not insist on its own rights or its
own way, for it is not self-seeking; it is not
touchy or fretful or resentful; it takes no
account of the evil done to it. [It pays no
attention to a suffered wrong.] It does not
rejoice at injustice and unrighteousness,
but rejoices when right and truth prevail.
Love bears up under anything and
everything that comes, is ever ready to
believe the best of every person, its hopes
are fadeless under all circumstances, and it
endures everything [without weakening].
Love never fails. [Never fades out or
becomes obsolete or comes to an end.]

1 Corinthians 13:4– 8 (Amplified Bible)

Do you want to know who God is and have a relationship with Him? If you do, love must be the main theme of your life. The more love you give, the more you understand God's heart and the more His voice becomes clearer and louder.

JOY

> *I have told you these things, that My joy and*
> *delight may be in you, and that your joy and*
> *gladness may be of full measure and complete*
> *and overflowing. This is My commandment:*
> *that you love one another as I have loved you.*

JOHN 15:11–12 (AMPLIFIED BIBLE)

You get to enjoy your life. More great news! Now you may ask this: How does this affect my relationship with God? Well, joy is one of those concepts that religious people often don't really get. There are all these religious teachings that state that you are not worthy of God's love and that you must suffer and be penitent for your mistakes. You see many people—not all of people, of course—going to church with their long faces in grief and mourning. When I was growing up, I remember hearing the old ladies in town say to the teenagers that if they went to the discotheque to dance, God would be angry at them. I got the impression that God was a cranky, old man. How ridiculous!

In reality, God created you to be happy. In God's first interaction with humans in the book of Genesis, He told them to go and be fruitful, multiply, fill the earth, subdue it, and have dominion over it. All of these words are political terms, powerful terms, and words of authority. God didn't tell them this: "I just created you so that you can struggle your whole life and suffer, and when you have suffered long enough, you will be a martyr for Me, and then I'll love you." Furthermore, if you read Genesis 2, God proceeds to tell them He has given them plants, fruits, animals, birds, fish, and resources for their benefit. He gave us domain over everything and anything that is in this world.

Believing that you're not allowed to have joy will change your relationship with God on a personal level. Yes, your relationship with God will grow if you remember to walk in love, pray to God, and connect with God, but God is so loving and merciful that you will get a lot out of these efforts. You get to enjoy your life!

Love and joy are deeply connected. If you are struggling to stay happy during the day, the fastest way to increase your happiness is to do something nice for someone else. Haven't you discovered that secret? I challenge you to try doing something kind for someone else.

You are going to run into different people almost every day of your life. Part of walking in love is to put smiles on people's faces. It can be something as simple as giving a compliment, or you may be divinely guided to give to someone in need. By doing so, you allow God's love to flow through you, thus increasing your understanding of who He is.

Here is another way to tune your spiritual ear: ask yourself repeatedly how you can be a blessing in someone else's life. God's answers will become easier to identify and hear.

You can accomplish powerful things with what you say. Words have profound impacts on people's brains. There is a huge difference between a child who is told every day how messy, lazy, and useless he or she is and a child who is told that he or she is smart, loved, and capable. Encouragement brings positive feelings and positive energy. Don't use your energy

Love that!

to judge and criticize other people's lives, even if they can't hear you. If you are honestly concerned about someone's attitude, you should consult God about it privately. If there is something to be done about it, God has full discretion to deal with the person directly or decide to use you or someone else to bring a word to that person, but you leave that to God. You may have good intentions in confronting someone, but that doesn't mean that that person is ready to hear what you have to say. You are not called to be God. You are called to love everyone. Be a blessing. Being judgmental and critical is the direct opposite of giving unconditional love.

Brutal!

It is easier to experience joy if you are speaking a positive message to others and to yourself. You don't need to ignore your problems, but neither do you need to talk about them over and over again with every person you meet.

PEACE

Blessed (enjoying, enviable happiness, spiritually prosperous—with joy and satisfaction in God's favor and salvation, regardless of their outward

> *conditions) are the makers and maintainers of*
> *peace, for they shall be called the sons of God!*

MATTHEW 5:9 (AMPLIFIED BIBLE)

Peace is very important. It allows you to enjoy your life. All of the fruits of the Holy Spirit come from love, and constantly practicing them will benefit your personal life and the people around you. We can say that practicing the fruits of the Holy Spirit is another way to say "I love you."

We are saying "I love you" because when we maintain emotional stability and consistency, we create a space of peace that is healing and enjoyable for the people around us. You can create peace wherever you are, but it is very important to keep peace in the home. Not only are you giving love when you create peace, but keeping the peace also creates an ideal environment for God's presence to flow and allows you to hear His voice more clearly.

God wants to give you gifts and blessings, but He is most interested in and impressed by your fruits. In His first conversation with Adam and Eve, God asks them to be fruitful. Having a relationship with God will allow you to live a more fulfilling life, but since you are called to be a blessing in the world and a light to the world, God may not allow you to hear His voice if you are not sharing love with those around you.

Stress from work, exhaustion, misunderstandings, voice tones, and defensiveness can create turmoil at home and disrupt the peace. Even if you are right that your spouse or kids should be better in a certain way, it is still your responsibility to choose a healthy emotional reaction to the circumstances. You are not God and are not able to fix everyone around you. You are called to keep the peace and allow God to work in that environment of peace.

You have learned that you are still human and that you still need to deal with your feelings of frustration, sadness, expectation, and hurt, but this doesn't mean that the people in your life are going to be mature enough to handle or understand your emotions. On the other hand, God is wise enough to understand you. You don't need to react and speak your mind in every circumstance. Instead, you should choose to keep the peace and bring your emotions and your questions to God. Not only have you kept the peace for those around you, but you have also kept your own peace, which makes it easier to hear the voice of God. He can then reveal to you your responsibility in whatever the circumstance is, and you can then ask for forgiveness, or He can deal with the other person or circumstance accordingly. You just let God be God. Peace will allow you to enjoy your life. Peace is the sign of God's will and presence.

There will be moments in your life when you will feel very unsure about making a decision. Having a personal relationship with God will grant you more guidance in these moments. However, you may sometimes feel like you're hearing mixed messages. In these cases, the decision that gives you more peace is the right decision. God works in light, truth, and love. Peace is the sign of God's approval. Peace signifies that God is leading your life.

Colossians 3:15 teaches that peace should be the umpire that settles your questions with finality. Sometimes, something will come up in your life that will sound good, and it may even be something you have wanted to do for a long time. It might even be a good thing, but somehow, you don't feel peaceful about doing this thing. You have to learn to leave it alone. Many of us have learned that the hard way. We have done something despite not feeling peaceful about it. Later, we find out the reason we shouldn't have done it in the first place.

There are people who feel that they always need to know the reason why they shouldn't do something. God may choose to tell you this reason, but if He doesn't, you need to have faith that God's will is perfect in your life. Maybe you will later understand why you had to decline a certain offer, but if you do not, just remember that nothing has more value than keeping the peace. In other words, it is never worth it to sacrifice your peace.

No matter what you are going through, you have the choice to maintain the peace. Many times, it is not the event itself that upsets us, but instead, it is not knowing how to *react* to that event that makes us upset. You can have peace even in the moments when your common sense tells you to be upset. As with the other fruits of the Holy Spirit, peace must be practiced over and over in your life. It is an exercise that will eventually become easy. As a result of this exercise, you'll start enjoying your life more, and making the decisions that keep the peace will become easy and natural.

Focusing on what is wrong with your circumstances is the main obstacle to achieving real peace. Having thoughts like "If I had a different job," or "If my spouse treated me better," or "If people would appreciate me more," or "If I had more money" will create a sense of frustration and a powerless spirit that will prevent peace from penetrating your life. Instead, you should share your frustrations with God and tell Him that you would like your circumstances to change. Your circumstances might not change instantly, but by communicating with God, you're making up your mind ahead of time to be peaceful. To help with this, you can also meditate on God and repeat to yourself that God loves you, that God appreciates you, that God is your provider, and that there is no question or concern that is too big for God. Make a habit of telling yourself these things several times a day.

First Peter 3 teaches that joy is released in our lives when we have peace, and this chapter names the types of peace we need to practice: peace with God, peace with our fellow humans, and finally peace with ourselves.

You need to be peaceful where you are in your life right now. Maybe you feel that you should have accomplished more than you have, or maybe you feel angry that you are having a hard time cultivating the fruits of the Holy Spirit in your life. If you feel this way, judging yourself won't bring you any closer to peace. If anything, worrying and criticizing yourself will make everything harder. Remember that you have access to God's *unconditional* love. When you judge yourself, remember what God feels about you. You can read the scriptures, and even better, you can ask this: "God, what do you think of me?"

You are loved. You are a work in progress that God will never give up on. It doesn't matter what you did. There is no hole so deep that God can't reach down and heal it. If God feels this way about us, who are we to judge ourselves?

Be a seeker, a creator, a keeper, and a follower of peace, and you will find God's presence and will.

PATIENCE

Cease from anger and forsake wrath; fret not yourself. (Do not be constantly or visibly worried or anxious.) It tends only to evil doing.

PSALM 37:8 (AMPLIFIED BIBLE)

Through God's love and grace, all of us have potential fruits of the Holy Spirit in the forms of seeds, so we need to exercise these fruits to let them grow in our lives. Since we are all wired differently, we all struggle in different areas. For me, patience is probably the fruit of the Holy Spirit that is the hardest to exercise.

I don't like waiting. I want everything done quickly and correctly. But this conflicts with God's character because although He is never late in coming into a person's life, it certainly doesn't seem—from a human perspective—that He is in any hurry to bring deliverance!

In my childhood, I spent a lot of time with my grandfather, who had this saying: "The time is the time—not before nor after." Every family trip or gathering was executed with military precision, and every meal was served at a specific time. It became part of my way of seeing the world. In my career, I had to deal with a lot of court appointments and hearings, and I always had deadlines. The clock ruled my life.

When I started dating Monica, who is now my wife, I developed very strong feelings for her very quickly. For over ten years, I had been praying to God to bring me the right partner. I had been dating for a long time, never finding any woman that would make me feel peaceful, until I met Monica. We both lived in Costa Rica at the time, and after some coffee dates, we finally agreed to take a trip to the beach. The day before the trip, we made a plan that I would pick her up early the next morning. When I showed up at the agreed time, she had just woken up. She was very happy to see me, but she was not ready at all. She began to talk, play music, pack snacks, and slowly gather all her things. She did every action with a lot of love and excitement for our trip, but my mind was focused on the fact that we should have already been on the road, so I couldn't really relax.

We finally left for the beach and spent some time there, and then I told her that I wanted to drive to a specific location to see the sunset. We started to drive, but she wanted to stop at stores and places along the way, and we ended up arriving too late for the sunset and could only enjoy about two minutes of it. In that moment, I remember thinking that she was disrespectful and couldn't commit to a plan, and I started talking with God in my head, saying, "Well, she is wonderful, but she clearly isn't the woman for me because that was rude." I went on and on with my judgments in my head. But when I stopped for a minute and looked at her, she seemed so happy and relaxed, and then she turned to me and told me that she was honored and happy to be there with me.

This confused me, as I believed it was not possible for her to be this happy when we clearly had missed most of the sunset and when the day had not gone as planned. So I prayed again, saying, "God, this surely cannot be the woman for me. She is not organized enough."

I heard God in my heart telling me this: "Stop complaining. You are in the right place with the right person, so you enjoy the moment and enjoy your life." It was in that instant that I realized that all of my judgments were in my head, but I couldn't really feel them in my heart. As I analyzed the trip, I realized that my heart had been peaceful all day, and it was my mental judgments that made me impatient and kept me from enjoying the day.

I do believe that sticking to your commitments is important, that being on time is respectful, and that my wife should honor agreements, but at that specific time in my life, those were not the lessons I needed on my personal path. I had to learn to slow down and enjoy life in the moment, and I had to learn to stop being so worried about the destination and enjoy the journey. I realized that for so many years, I had been so impatient to reach my goals that I hadn't really enjoyed much of anything. There was always something to do. I was so determined to finish high school and college, build my career, and buy a car and a house that I never really enjoyed anything because I wasn't where I wanted to be yet.

My lack of patience had hindered my joy for life, and my wife was the person that God chose to use as an instrument to heal that area of my life. God knew exactly what I needed, and in my impatience, I was getting ready to discard her! All because a couple of things had not gone according to my expectation of how things should be done.

You should not feel guilty when you feel impatience, but as with the rest of your emotions, you need to learn to not act on your impatience. Instead, you should bring your concerns, doubts, and questions to God in your prayers. I didn't know I could share my frustrations with God, and I wasted years of my life being unhappy.

This was very important for me to understand because I had been taught that God was mighty and that He cared for me. I had also been taught that I could ask for anything that I wanted in Jesus's name, and I would receive it. Yet from my vantage point, there was a lot of "asking" happening on my part, and I couldn't see all of the results. This made me resentful because

I thought that God had the power to do wonders but was not very interested in doing anything for me.

But this was obviously not true. I can now look back on my life with the knowledge of God's will and understand why things happened the way they did and why it was for the better. Jesus explained this principle to His disciples. He used the example of a woman in labor who has no choice but to go through all of the pain of labor. But when it is over, she doesn't even think about the pain anymore. Instead, she rejoices in seeing her baby. Of course, it was going to take time for me to finish my degrees, build my career, and find a wife, but I wanted everything immediately, so I was more interested in changing my circumstances than enjoying the present blessings.

Maybe you are a person who does not struggle with patience. Maybe you are patient and peaceful all the time. But if you are not, hopefully you will eventually get a handle on your impatience once you have practiced over and over. But in the meantime, remember that patience comes from love and that love comes from God, so the best thing that you can do is pray to God and ask for some patience.

We need to have patience with other people, since being patient is another way to give love. Many times, we lose our patience with people in the areas where we are strong or gifted. Sooner or later, you will come across someone who is not handling things the way you would have, and your immediate reaction will be frustration and criticism. But thinking negative things or saying things like, "How could you be so slow?" or "How did you do that wrong? It's so easy! It took me minutes to do the same thing!" is just hurtful and useless. Even if you are right that there is a better way to get something done, you could voice your opinion with love and as a suggestion. Losing your patience doesn't do that person any good, nor does losing your patience strengthen your relationship with God. On the contrary, God gets upset when you are impatient with and judgmental of other people, since it is God who has made you talented in the areas you are criticizing others. Be generous, give advice, and be compassionate when others are having a hard time with a task.

I insist that to give love is to speak God's language. If you are patient with people, they will be patient with you, and by giving this form of love, you will gain a more intimate connection with God. Remember that you're not the only one of God's children who is trying to learn about Him and grow closer to Him. When you lose your patience and start criticizing others, especially your brothers and sisters in the faith, you are stunting their growth and the work that God has been doing in their lives.

The minute you lose your patience, you give in to your emotions and start making decisions and saying things that you shouldn't. People around you will get hurt by your decisions and words, and then you will spend a lot of time and energy on either apologizing and trying to fix the mess you created or trying to defend your position. That energy is better spent in conversation with God or in meditation on God's voice. You could have prevented the whole thing if you had been patient. Remember that God called you to be a light to the world.

Kindness

> *Be kind and do good [doing favors so that*
> *someone derives benefit from them] and lend,*
> *expecting and hoping for nothing in return*
> *but considering nothing as lost and despairing*
> *of no one; and then your recompense (your*
> *reward) will be great (rich, strong, intense, and*

*abundant), and you will be sons of the Most
High, for He is kind and charitable and good.*

LUKE 6:35 (AMPLIFIED BIBLE)

To be kind is to be generous, warm, considerate, and giving to others. All of the fruits of the Holy Spirit are interconnected. When you start to seek your relationship with God, all of your fruits of the Holy Spirit are still seeds. They need to be planted, watered, and nurtured. As you practice each of your fruits each day, you are letting that particular seed grow more and more in your life, but you are also allowing the other fruits of the Holy Spirit to grow as well. For example, when you have peace, it is easier to have patience. Kindness allows you to find joy easily in your life and also gives you perspective.

Let's face it—we might have the desire to deepen our relationships with God, but we are still humans, and there are some days that we just don't feel like doing anything to strengthen our relationships with God. I have found that when you are having a hard time exercising the fruits of the Holy Spirit, being kind to someone allows you to become immediately grounded. There is an instant release of joy in your life when you manage to put a smile on someone else's face and when you allow love to flow through you, which will inspire you to continue exercising the rest of the fruits of the Holy Spirit.

There are multiple records of God commanding people to be good to one another in the scriptures: honor your parents, do good to your neighbors, and feed the widows and the orphans. Even though it is a command, as with everything that God asks from us, there are rewards when we do it. When you practice any of the fruits of the Holy Spirit, you create a better life for yourself and the people around you. For example, when you are peaceful, your family feels more relaxed at home. It is the same way with kindness— God has promised that being kind will bring financial and material blessings into your life.

In the town that I grew up in, there was a luxurious house on a hill that I passed every day on my way to work. I was always curious about it, and I would even fantasize about how beautiful it must be on the inside and how stunning its views were. One day, it turned out that the owner needed an appraisal of the house for a possible sale, so the owner contacted our firm. I went to the property and met the owner. His wife and kids were at the house, and they seemed very unhappy and stressed. The owner wasn't very pleasant. He was cursing and was criticizing the maid and his wife in front of my coworker and me. He didn't seem to be a successful businessman. Right before I left, I asked him how he had made his money. He told me that he had inherited a beautiful beach property in Uvita, Costa Rica, from his grandfather and had sold it for thousands of dollars. Then I finished the inspection and left the house.

I got in my car and drove away feeling very frustrated. I was discouraged because I felt that I was working hard at my job and at being a good person, and this man I had just met seemed so critical and bitter, but he had a beautiful home. I started praying, which sounded more like complaining. I said, "God, why don't I have a wealthy inheritance?" As I was sharing my frustration with God and feeling that life was unfair, I remembered Romans 8, which says that we are heirs with God. Then I heard God's voice telling me this: "I am your inheritance! I am your 'beach property.'"

God began to teach me about prosperity, and the first lesson about prosperity was to be kind. He prompted

Marcos Borges

me to help my mother, brother, sister, nieces, and nephews financially. I even helped with fund raisers, bringing food to church activities and to people in need. God showed me that He was going to prosper me so that I could take care of others. Remember that God works individually and that your path might be different than mine, but I share that God prospers me more each year as a testimony. He has shown me the truth about kindness, and I have done my best to hear when God wants me to reach out and give.

Kindness can be given in more than just material ways. You can also do kind deeds, give kind words, and give love and patience with a kind heart. Regardless of the way that you give kindness, remember that you must do it without expecting anything in return, as Jesus taught in Luke 6. If you give kindness and expect something in return, and if your expectation is not met, you will turn your blessings and joy into hurt and disappointment. Being kind is a privilege because you get to experience one of God's traits. When you practice kindness, you can begin to understand how God feels and acts toward other people and how He feels about you. It is like looking at the world through God's eyes. As a result of being kind, your relationship and connection with God will grow. God wants to improve and bless your life, and one of the main ways He blesses you is by using you as a tool to bless other people. If you want to learn to hear God's voice, pay special attention to what you can do for the people around you.

Whatever you focus your attention on will grow in your life. If you focus on trying to change the people around you, people will think you are controlling. If you focus on getting things for yourself, you will become exponentially selfish. The way you exercise kindness is by constantly thinking about being kind. Make kindness your purpose. You can even plan ahead. Every night, you can meditate about a kind thing you can do or say to your spouse or to those you interact with the next day. If you can't come up with something, ask God! This is yet another great exercise in learning to hear His voice.

Plan ahead to encourage someone; to say something nice to someone; and to be grateful to your hairdresser, to your clerk, and to anyone you are going to see during your day.

Plan ahead to be kind and rewarding. There will always be little things that your spouse or your kids will do repeatedly that make you lose your peace. It may be one of the kids not kissing you good-bye, not putting the toilet seat down, or not cleaning up after himself or herself. There will always be something that bugs you. Instead of being someone who uses that knowledge to build up anger and an attitude of "I told you so," use it to plan ahead to be forgiving when something irritating happens. God will talk to you loudly and clearly, but it is up to you to act on His voice. Having a personal relationship with God means inviting Him into every single event of your life, and His presence helps make you kind.

Exercise kindness, and be a giver of forgiveness. You will not only put a smile on God's face, but you will also bring peace and joy into your home and into all of your personal relationships.

GOODNESS

Stand therefore [hold your ground], having tightened the belt of truth around your loins and having put on the breastplate of integrity and of moral rectitude and right standing with God.

EPHESIANS 6:14 (AMPLIFIED BIBLE)

Goodness is a virtue. It means to be in good standing with God and to be righteousness before Him. Goodness comes from love because when you really understand how deep and unconditional God's love for you is, you will be freed from any judgment against yourself. Goodness brings the freedom to live your life lovingly and to accept who and how you are at any moment. You are forgiven by grace, and to practice goodness is to understand that through grace you are in right standing with God.

Paul wrote letters of instruction to many ancient churches. In these letters, he repeatedly taught people to "put on" the spiritual clothing of love, faith, peace, and righteousness. Putting on these things means that you have to do them daily, just as you put on your normal clothing daily.

If you don't remind yourself that you are righteous before God, you may feel overwhelmed by your doubts and fears, and you may be discouraged from seeking a relationship with Him.

You may understand how you should behave and how the fruits of the Holy Spirit operate, but you may still react emotionally in some situations and hurt other people or yourself. If this happens, do not lose perspective. Remember that God can help you repair anything, that God is love, and that the fruits of the Holy Spirit are gifts that He gives to you, since all of them are traits of His personality.

To learn about the fruits of the Holy Spirit and their real power, I had to spend years letting God love me and show me how to be joyful, how to receive His peace and patience in my mistakes, and how to receive His kindness in the forms of the blessings and gifts that He bestowed on me.

If you never learn to receive God's kindness and mercy for yourself, you won't be able to give His kindness to other people. This goes for all the fruits of the Holy Spirit. You can't give away what you don't have. This is why the fruits of the Holy Spirit are so deeply connected to your relationship with God.

Free yourself, forgive yourself, and let yourself be in good standing with God. God is not a tough task-master. He is merciful, kind, and good, and He is easy to have a relationship with. He educates us with love and kindness, and He doesn't punish you immediately when you make a mistake. Instead, He comforts you and provides you with a second—or third or fourth— chance and helps you correct any mistakes and messes that you have made.

Punishing and reproving yourself does not enrich your life. Without feeling God's righteousness, you will give in to fear and anger. Have you considered if you are hard to get along with? Not feeling good about yourself leads to a never-ending cycle: if you don't love yourself, you can't love others. Then people will label you as harsh or bitter, and then their judgment will make you feel worse about yourself. The cycle can go on and on. But God doesn't say this about you! He says that you are free of judgment and that you are loved and understood. You might even feel that being in this cycle is not your fault. You may feel that people were just constantly reproving you, and then it became part of your character. However, even if you didn't create it, it is your responsibility to remind yourself who you are before God.

Relationships and life are complicated, but it doesn't do you any good to be bitter and resentful and to let circumstances harden your heart, make you mean toward others, and create barriers against love. Rise above these lies, and "put on" God's righteousness (several times a day if you need to). Tell yourself this: "I am loved. I am good. I am taken care of." Talk to God, and tell Him when you are feeling chastised or excluded. Let His voice tell you that you are loved.

I challenge you to expect God's goodness, blessings, and kindness in your life every day.

FAITHFULNESS

> *If we are faithless [do not believe and are untrue to Him], He remains true (faithful to His Word and His righteous character), for He cannot deny Himself.*

2 TIMOTHY 2:13 (AMPLIFIED BIBLE)

To be faithful means to be true to your promises and vows and to be reliable or trustworthy. As with the rest of the fruits of the Holy Spirit, when you receive God's faithfulness to you, you can also practice it in your personal life.

We see in the scriptures that God is who He is. He is faithful and loving, and even when we fail, doubt, or give in to our emotions, He remains faithful to us.

In the journey of having a relationship with God, knowing this takes most of the pressure off of us. God knows who we are, and He does not demand that we perform perfectly at all times. He expects you to grow, but that is so He can bring bigger blessings into your life. He does not expect you to grow so that He can love you more. You already have all of God's love.

It is very important to understand faithfulness as a part of God's character because this understanding will free you from religion. Some religions tell you that you have to go through all sorts of steps, rules, and rituals to be in good standing with God, and some religions will make you feel like a sinner all the time. Many people who pursue a relationship with God give up on this pursuit and stop talking with Him because they feel embarrassed or ashamed because of some of their actions. A religion might tell you that you are not worthy to talk to God, but love, grace, and faithfulness say otherwise because God "cannot deny Himself." He can't stop loving you! He can't stop himself from wanting to bless you and have a relationship with you.

When you study Jesus's life, you find that He was constantly giving love to people. He was constantly talking to and helping everyone—from the average person to those who were excluded by society, like prostitutes, adulteresses, and gentiles. The only people who Jesus got truly angry with were the religious people. Jesus explains how their practices pushed people further away from Him instead of bringing people closer to Him. Who would want to have a relationship with a God who is always angry and judgmental?

The faithfulness that we receive from God is a beautiful gift and another manifestation of God's true and unconditional love for us. It doesn't matter what you do. He is who He is, and He will always love you and keep His promises to look after you. There are even people who receive promises from God and step away from having a connection with Him, yet God still fulfills His promises in their lives!

You should apply faithfulness by realizing that you have to stop letting what other people do, or don't do, change you. You have to make up your mind that you are going to work on your relationship with God, maintain your communication with Him, and give and receive love, joy, peace, patience, kindness, and humility at all times. You should do all of these things not only when you are getting good responses from people or when things are easy but also when life is hard.

Be determined to be all that God wants you to be, regardless of the results that you are getting. For example, you may have to be kind and loving toward a mean person for a long time before you see any positive results, but you shouldn't be kind with the expectation of that person changing in an instant and then behaving differently. You should be kind because it allows you to practice love, which enhances and deepens your relationship with God. In fact, these are exactly the types of circumstances that are best for practicing the fruits of the Holy Spirit. If you feel that it is getting too hard and that people are mistreating you, you should bring your sadness to God and allow Him to be your comforter and healer. This will also be an exercise than enhances your communication with Him.

God is the author and finisher of your faith. He never starts things without finishing them. If you asked for a relationship with Him and began this process, He will complete it. At the same time, you also need to finish what you start. Be reliable, and be faithful.

Gentleness

For the body does not consist of one limb or organ but of many. If the foot should say, "Because I am not the hand, I do not belong to the body, would it be therefore not of the body?" If the ear should say, "Because I am not the eye, I do not belong to the body, would it be therefore not of the body?" If the whole body were an eye, where [would be the sense of] hearing? If the whole body were an ear, where [would be the sense of] smell? But as it is, God has placed and arranged the limbs and organs in the body, each [particular one] of them, just as He wished and saw fit and with the best adaptation.

1 Corinthians 12:14–18 (Amplified Bible)

Gentleness means the quality of being humble and meek. This fruit of the Holy Spirit might take a lot of work to develop, but it is incredibly rewarding. A humble person is a happy person because he or she is freed from judgment, from trying to impress people, and from being a hypocrite or a pretender. Humility brings a freedom that allows you to have peace within yourself. You don't need to compete with anyone. Instead, you can be confident in who you are and what you know, and you can become aware of the things that you don't know without feeling that you need to be something or someone else to meet other people's expectations.

In my career, I have had the opportunity to provide legal services to many clients from a variety of socioeconomic backgrounds—from farmers who are dealing with issues with the government and environmental rights to wealthy people who are buying luxurious properties. I remember one case that particularly impacted me. A new and extremely wealthy client wanted to buy a property in Costa Rica to design a resort and condominium development. The property was in a remote location in the mountains, and during the development of the project, there was an issue with accessing the property. The developer wanted to expand the road, and to do so, it was necessary to cut some trees and build over some farmland. During the mediation and negotiation meetings with the farmers and the developer, I noticed that even though the developer had been very clear that he was willing to modify the path to the road to harm fewer trees, the farmers didn't seem to acknowledge that he was open to a discussion. For many days, the meetings consisted of listening to the farmers complain about the economy and the politicians. They made derogatory comments—such as "People with money are so selfish and think that they can do whatever they want"—instead of trying to find a solution. By the end of the meetings, the developer was very frustrated and impatient as well and would say equally offensive things, such as, "These people are so ignorant and uneducated."

After several days, an agreement was finally reached. On the same day, I was driving with the developer to his house to sign some final documents. We stopped in a supermarket on the way, and as he was picking up some produce, he looked at me and said, "I'm glad that I can get my produce here and that I don't have to deal with those farmers." Then God said to me, "How does he think the produce got there in the first place?"

It made me think that that is a simple life lesson that most of us know on the surface but don't meditate deeply on. For years, I had heard farmers complain about politicians, the government, and investors, but I realized that even if some officials were corrupt, corruption is not always the case, and entrepreneurs are necessary to create jobs, boost the economy, and collect taxes. At the same time, farmers and other service providers are a blessing. They harvest food for all of us and provide us with services that make us feel comfortable while dining or vacationing. They are truly a blessing! It almost makes you feel that God in His wisdom created life in a balance that reminds us that we are all part of the same body. We all need one another, and we must be humble enough to recognize that dependence. The Bible says that all of us are a part of the body of Christ. As a body, we all need each other.

If this applies to our daily, earthly lives, it also applies to our spiritual lives. If you are a truly humble person, you can find happiness and peace wherever you are in life. It does not matter if you are the best musician on earth or a janitor. You do not put your self-worth and value in your profession, even if your job is seen as a "lowly" job. There is no such thing as a "lowly" job. If you are a humble person, your joy comes from doing what God is asking you to do. God can certainly help you change your life circumstances, and you can tell Him what you would like to do with your life. He will help you reach your goals, but in your growth process, God may require you to stay in a certain place in your life for a while. In this time, humility is the ally that will allow you to be patient and learn what you need to learn. God has everything under control, and He anoints and equips us all in different ways. God doesn't see the world as we see it. We think that there are positions that are more exalted than others, but God made us all a part of the same body.

I believe many people have misjudged the real power of meekness. Many people think that if they are meek, they will be abused or stepped on by everyone else. But that is not true. The word *meekness* comes from the Greek word *praus*, which was the word used for a beast that had been tamed. For thousands of years, humans have been capable of raising and taming animals that are far stronger than we are: horses, dogs, lions, and even elephants. My family and I have a professionally trained attack dog named Hruby. Our dog has protected us many times, even against armed people. But whenever a family member or I chastise her, she doesn't retaliate, despite the fact that she could do some serious damage or even kill us. It amazes my wife and me that Hruby behaves differently with different people. She plays more aggressively with our fourteen-year-old son, but when she plays with our five-year-old niece, Hruby is so gentle. She moves slowly, does not pull hard on the toys, and doesn't bark. We know that she will never hurt any of us because of the love that she has for our family. To have your strength under control is true meekness.

You are not giving away your power by being humble. It is quite the opposite. You are growing in your power. There might be times where you know that you could do something to get back at someone that wronged you, but you choose not to do it because you don't feel that is what God wants you to do. In fact, it takes more courage and bravery to wait on God than to act emotionally and scream and trample all over people. Even if you know that someone is wrong or has misjudged you, you are not called to correct everything and everyone. Let God deal with it.

Humility allows you to recognize that although you have knowledge or wisdom in an area that another person doesn't, you can still be patient and love that person where he or she is in his or her own growth process. God loves these people and is patient with them, so why wouldn't you be? And if they are truly mistreating you, let God be your healer and vindicator.

Humility also works the other way around. It might be that someone knows something better than you do, and being humble allows you to hear that person without having to feel defensive or criticized. Let's study Philippians 2:3–5, which says, "Do nothing from factional motives [through contentiousness, strife, selfishness, or unworthy ends] or prompted by conceit and empty arrogance. Instead, in the true spirit of humility (lowliness of mind) let each regard the others as better than and superior to himself [thinking more highly of one another than you do of yourselves]. Let each of you esteem and look upon and be concerned for not his own interests, but also each for the interests of others. Let this same attitude and purpose and mind be in you that was in Christ."

Let's clarify that this doesn't mean that you should think badly of yourself. Paul says to have an "open heart" to hear other people. If we are all one body with different roles, functions, and individual personalities, and if God is an individual God who reveals Himself to all of us in different ways, then we all have something to learn from everyone else. Are you open to receiving a word of advice or a word of correction? Are you open to hearing your spouse, partner, or friend tell you that maybe you didn't handle or react to a situation very well?

It might feel scary to have this level of openness in your heart, but you should not be concerned because you can always share whatever people tell you with God in prayer and hear what God has to say about it too. He might agree, or He might disagree. The Bible teaches us to hear from everyone and to retain the good and discard the bad.

In the scriptures, there is a story where God speaks to a prophet through a donkey. So isn't it feasible that God would talk to you through someone who loves you?

A person with a humble attitude is willing to receive and learn and does not think that he or she is more important than someone else. Humility allows you to tell people what your strengths and weakness are without feeling embarrassed or condemned, especially since every person has weaknesses.

SELF-CONTROL

Whatever may be your task, work at it
heartily (from the soul), as [something done]
for the Lord and not for men, knowing

[with all certainty] that it is from the Lord
[and not from men] that you will receive
the inheritance which is your reward.

COLOSSIANS 3:23–24 (AMPLIFIED BIBLE)

Love is the source of all of the fruits of the Holy Spirit. Joy, peace, patience, kindness, goodness, faithfulness, and gentleness are stages or different manifestations of what love is. If you allow yourself to receive love from God, you will love yourself and give love to others, and then all of the fruits of the Holy Spirit will start to develop and grow in your life. Love is the beginning of everything, but self-control is what keeps all of the pieces together.

Learning to have self-control might be a painful process because it forces you to look at yourself intently. Often when someone is being confronted about a hurtful thing that he or she has done or said, that person excuses himself or herself with thoughts like "This is who I am," "I am too old to change," or "I just can't help it. I can't control myself." The first thing you need to understand is that this is a false statement. You can control yourself if you really want to. That is the key: you must want to. Self-control has to be important to you. Remember that a relationship with God is meant to bless your life and the lives of others, so God has no use for someone who is capable of hearing His voice clearly but who chooses to ignore it. There is no point in a person having prophetic gifts if that person will not watch the way he or she behaves and won't give love to others or be a blessing to the world.

We may understand love perfectly, but that doesn't mean that we always want to share it with others. There are some mornings that you just get up on the wrong side of the bed. Perhaps there is someone in your life who disappoints you in the same area repeatedly, so you don't feel very patient or loving toward that person. But we have the power in us to put on love and mercy. True love is unconditional. Even if you don't feel like loving that person, you have self-control and do it out of your love for God.

Loving God is possibly the biggest motivation to keep control of your emotions, thoughts, and judgments. My father abandoned my family when I was a kid, and it was very painful for all of us because he had been cheating on my mother for a while. Before he fled the country so that he wouldn't have to pay child support, he gave all of our family's money to his mistress. He also mortgaged our house and kept the money. Without any money left in her accounts, my mother couldn't pay the mortgage back. In a matter of weeks, we had lost our father, our home, our money, and our stability. It was a very hard time for my family, which we only survived through the love and faithfulness of God and His daily miracles.

My family worked hard for nine years to regain our stability, and then my father returned to the country because the child-support payments had expired. He filed a lawsuit against my mother and me based on a claim of domestic violence against my younger sister. We were shocked. He, of course, lost the case, but I was angry and full of hate and resentment toward him. He had abandoned us and then put us through the stress of a lawsuit just when we were starting to get back on our feet, and the worst part was that he never apologized. However, I was raised as a Christian, and I wanted to get rid of that hate in my heart because carrying that resentment was just painful.

After praying and trying to forgive him for a long time, I started to feel that I could never forgive him or talk to him. It wasn't until one day that I read Ephesians 5 and 6, where Paul talks about loving, respecting, and being submissive to other people and doing it as a service to the Lord, that I began to heal. I asked God this: "So I have to forgive him not because he has earned it but because of you?" God told me this: "Yes, in fact, if you stay angry at him, you are just going to make it harder for him to ever repent and heal from what he has done."

Who was I to decide if someone deserved to heal or not? Since then, God has had me talk to him, check on him, and go out to have coffee with him. And I still struggle with doing these things because he still has not apologized. In fact, sometimes I have to sit through entire conversations and listen to him blame my mother and us for what he did. In my flesh, I don't feel like having any compassion or patience for him, but because of my love for God and His command to be a light in the world, I try to love my father. Maybe I will be the instrument that God will use to heal him, but maybe I will not be. But I still try to fulfill my obligation to love. I think that we love God in stages. When you are trying to have a relationship with God and hear His voice, you will begin to love Him more and be willing to go the extra mile for Him.

Self-control will add power to your life and your relationship with God. Begin to do what you are supposed to do as a service to the Lord, not because you feel like it or want to do it. Self-control is your friend and your ally. Be thankful that God has put a seed of self-control in your life so that you don't have to give in to your fears, anger, and emotions but can instead choose to do what is right, even when you don't feel like it. The Bible teaches that we are God's representatives on earth and that the way we represent Him is by choosing to give love.

God is our father, and as a father, He won't give us responsibilities that we are not ready to handle. God loves us and cares for us, and He will not put us in situations where we can damage our relationships with Him or others. As believers, we like to hear what God can do for us, but we don't like to hear what our part is. So know that to achieve a deeper relationship with God and to be able to hear His voice in a more powerful way, you have to make a constant effort to practice self-control and all of the fruits of the Holy Spirit. Without that effort, we will begin to drift, either giving in to our self-judgment and impatience or becoming full of pride because we think we are better and holier than others because we have heard the voice of God. Acting this way will discourage your peers who are seeking the same path.

The scriptures teach that pride is an abomination in the eyes of God and that pride is the original sin. There is a law that states that everyone has the right to do whatever they want unless their actions interfere with the freedom and rights of others. For example, you have the right to play music at your home, but you don't have the right to play music in someone else's house without that person's permission since that person has a right to privacy. This is why pride is such an abomination—because when you are prideful, you are impacting the rights of the people around you. Your pride impacts, among other things, their right to be forgiven, their right to be loved, and their right to receive patience; since God is the judge of all the earth and since He cannot deny Himself, your pride brings consequences upon yourself as well.

It is an even bigger responsibility when you have a deeper knowledge of who God is and can hear His voice, since your pride will stop the flow of God's power through you. You could be preventing blessings and healing from entering the lives of the people around you. We all have to deal with pride. Even the disciples—who had witnessed Jesus's power and wisdom—were worried about who was going to be the next leader after Jesus was gone! Jesus told them that the person who was a servant to others was going to be the biggest person in the kingdom of God. In other words, Jesus asked them to serve people, and the way we serve people is by giving them love. Self-control reminds us to be loving and meek.

One of the first signs that you are losing your self-control is when you begin to criticize. Maybe you are in a situation at work where you feel that your boss doesn't really know what he or she is doing. Maybe you are having a hard time being patient with him or her, and it is getting hard for you to keep your joy at work. Instead of sitting down with some coworkers and criticizing your boss, try praying for your boss. Maybe no one has ever prayed for him or her, and maybe God wants to use you. Set a personal goal to grow your relationship with God. When you feel like criticizing or complaining, pray instead.

Ask God every morning to give you self-control. I'm not suggesting that you should change your morning dynamic or that you should get up earlier to pray for one hour if you don't want to, but you should pray for at least five minutes. While you are in the shower, ask God to help you keep your emotions under control. Ask Him to remind you to love your family and coworkers. If you begin to do this, I can almost promise you that you will notice growth in your relationship with God. And if you fail to keep your emotions in check, remember God's goodness, forgive yourself, and keep on loving. Be consistent, and be faithful.

Colossians 3:14 says to "put on" love. To "put on" is an action, not a feeling. It is a decision. Don't just wish that you would feel more loving. You must decide to be loving. Every day, make a plan ahead of time. Say this to yourself: "I am going to go out into the world and be a blessing. I am going to encourage people. I'm going to put a smile on someone's face. If I see a need, I am going to try to meet that need. I am going to give love!"

CHAPTER 4

Trusting God

§

Fear not [there is nothing to fear], for I am
with you; do not look around you in terror
and be dismayed, for I am your God. I will
strengthen and harden you to difficulties,
yes, I will help you; yes, I will hold you
up and retain you with My [victorious]
right hand of rightness and justice

ISAIAH 41: 10 (AMPLIFIED BIBLE)

TRUSTING IN GOD CAN BE the biggest challenge for
those who want to hear His voice and have an intimate, personal relationship with Him. Hopefully, it
is easy for you, but in my experience, trusting Him
is in the advanced level, so I warn you that it might

be easier to read about trust in this book than to go out and actually do it. But you *can* do it, and now you know how to have the self-control to do it.

There are two reasons why I believe trust is hard to achieve. First, God asks people to do things that they don't want to do. God might ask you to leave a relationship, to ask for forgiveness from someone you hurt, or to forgive someone who really damaged you, and you really won't want to do those things. Second, people don't like to depend on anyone else.

It might be very scary to forgive and let things go or to stop behaving certain way or change things, especially because many people build their entire reality and personality around something that happened to them. For example, perhaps you were mistreated in your relationships for a long time, and you built up a barrier that is now a part of your personality. Perhaps you said this: "I won't ever trust anyone." Or maybe you have been in an abusive, dysfunctional relationship for a long time, and you are unhappy, but you don't know how to leave. Traumas and life events can create fears or buttons that can be pushed at different moments in your life. We can carry around baggage with us for so long that we can't even imagine who we would be without it. On top of our fears, we inherently don't like to rely on anyone. We all prefer to be self-sufficient. For this reason, when you grow in your relationship with God and you begin to get deeper with Him, He might ask you to change some things and let go of other things that you might not really want to let go of. God knows what is best for us, but do we really trust Him?

Let's read what Paul wrote in 2 Corinthians 12:7–9:

> To keep me from being puffed up and too much elated by the exceeding greatness (preeminence) of these revelations, there was given me a thorn (a splinter) in the flesh, to rack and buffet and harass me, to keep me from being excessively exalted. Three times I called upon the Lord and besought [Him] about this and begged that it might depart from me; But He said to me, No; My grace (My favor and loving-kindness and mercy) is enough for you [sufficient against any danger and enables you to bear the trouble manfully]; for My strength and power are made

perfect (fulfilled and completed) and show
themselves most effective in weakness.

(Amplified Bible)

Paul's story is extraordinary. God used Paul more
mightily than anyone else around. Paul went from
persecuting believers to having a miraculous conver-
sion. While you and I study and read books, Paul received a deep knowledge of love and grace through a
direct revelation from God. He wrote the most beautiful and complete texts about love and mercy that
we have in the Bible. He wrote the majority of the
New Testament in the Bible. This man—who had all
this understanding, could clearly hear God's voice,
and spent his life sharing his knowledge—tells the
Corinthians that he has an extreme pain in his body
and that when he begged God to take it away from
him, God said no!

We like to think that God will do everything that
we want, but although He will hear our requests, He
will sometimes say to us, "No, it is more valuable to
Me that you stay in that situation than get out of it."
He said to Paul, "My grace and My strength will be
sufficient for you." In other words, God sometimes

says this to us: "I am allowing you to suffer because there is something that you need to learn. You need to trust that My decision is for your own good and benefit and that I am not leaving you alone. I am here to hear you, and My power will be with you as you face your trial."

We like to do everything ourselves, but we need God. Some people don't like that. They want it their way. The Bible teaches us to seek God, to worship God with gratitude, and to make God a part of everything in our lives. One time in law school, I heard one of my classmates say that he did not believe in what he called the "Bible God" because that God was so egotistical that He would only bless those who worshiped Him. It turned out that my classmate had never read the Bible and had just heard a couple of sermons from one preacher, but he dared to have an opinion as if he were an expert. I believe that many people feel this way. But what God is really saying is this: "You cannot have a fulfilling life without love, and I *am* love. All the love of the universe comes from and flows from Me, so you need to seek love in order to gain power in your life and enjoy it!" Christ said that away from God, you can do nothing. This is not because of God's ego but because He is the source of all power. Here is a simple analogy: You can't fill your car with gas while it's sitting in your garage, no matter how badly you'd like to. Ultimately, you are going to have to go to a gas station or a refinery to get fuel. In the same way, God is the source of love, and you must go to Him for it!

Without love, we can't be happy. And this goes beyond romantic love. We need to have love in every area of our lives—love for family, friends, work, home, and God. And we need to feel loved and appreciated in return.

Love is the internal connection between our spirits and God. Most of the time, we experience this connection naturally, but we need to learn to identify it for what it is. Every time you give or allow yourself to receive love, you have connected with God. Every time you tell your children that you love them, God is flowing through you. Every time that you pet a cute dog and it brings you joy, God is flowing through you. Every time you are grateful for your food, you tell God that you love Him and are grateful for Him. Every time you express how beautiful a flower or sunset is, you are connecting to God and thanking Him for His creativity. Every time someone says something like "I love you" or "You are smart," that is God talking to you through that person. And every time a family member hurts you and you forgive him or her, God flows through you!

We sometimes connect with God in our lives without even noticing! Using the power of self-control, you can encourage these behaviors and make yourself loving every day. I promise you that this is true: if you do this over and over and over, you will know God and who He is, and you will hear His voice. All the paths of love lead to God.

GOD GETS IT

People do not like to give away their power. Once you understand that God is there for you and that He really wants the best for you and educates you so you can get greater blessings in life, it is easier to give in to Him and have more peace when you are going through tough times.

The deeper your relationship with God gets, the more He pushes you to heal deep triggers and wounds. The scriptures explain this process with the metaphor of refining gold through fire. This is another scripture that is often misunderstood by religious people. They believe it means that we need to suffer or be punished, but that is not what God wants for us or does to us. He wants you to be a healed and complete person. God knows that the healing process is painful for us, but that process is not a punishment, a waste of time, or a test to earn God's love.

To heal, we must face ourselves and our fears, let go of the past, forgive ourselves and the people who hurt us, and ask for forgiveness from those we hurt. All these actions can be really painful. God also pushes us to deal with our lives, and we do not always want to do this because it will have painful consequences, just as leaving dysfunctional relationships or changing our impulses to control everything can have painful consequences. It is hard because we don't want to get hurt, so we use the excuse that God doesn't really get it so that we don't have to do it. For example, God might be asking you to forgive your abusive parents and care for them, or God might be asking you to forgive your ex-partner. But you really don't want to. Your emotional response is to feel that God must be wrong or that He is clearly not taking your feelings into consideration. Every time we feel misunderstood, we say things like, "You just don't get it," "You weren't there," or "Walk a mile in my shoes." I have even heard people say this: "God is safe up there, while I am struggling down here, so why do I have to listen to Him?"

But this excuse doesn't apply to God, because the fact is that He does get it, even if you feel that what He is asking you to do is not related to what you are praying for. Maybe you are praying for a promotion at work, but God is asking you to forgive and reconnect with your family. You may ask this: What does my family have to do with my career? Well, maybe if you were to get a promotion, you would become so busy and would begin traveling or doing other things that you would never get time to reconnect with your family. Even if your story is different than the previous example, the point is that God gets it.

Let's read Luke 23:39–43:

> One of the criminals who was suspended kept up a railing at Him, saying, "Are You not the Christ (the Messiah)? Rescue Yourself and us!" But the other one reproved him, saying, "Do you not even fear God, seeing you yourself are under the same sentence of condemnation and suffering the same penalty? And we indeed

suffer it justly, receiving the due reward
of our actions; but this Man has done
nothing out of the way [nothing strange,
eccentric, perverse, or unreasonable]."
Then he said to Jesus, "Lord, remember
me when You come in Your kingly
glory!" And He answered him, "Truly I
tell you, today you shall be with Me."

(AMPLIFIED BIBLE)

The two thieves that were crucified with Jesus represent very well the different reactions that we can have. The most common reaction is the reaction of the first thief. There was a divinely guided purpose for Christ's suffering, yet the thief's response was this: "Don't you have the power to do something about it?" Does that response sound familiar? When you go through something that is painful, do you come to God with a resentful attitude instead of a patient one? You may ask these questions: Aren't You powerful? Why am I here? It is not easy to stop yourself from asking these questions, and God is faithful, so He will deliver you sooner or later. So why be unhappy during the whole process?

Again, it is hard not to feel this way, but you can use your self-control to remind yourself of God's love and faithfulness. "Put on" peace and patience! You have the power to see your circumstances as the second thief did. Let's read again what he said: "Do you not even fear God, seeing you yourself are under the same sentence of condemnation and suffering the same penalty?" In other words, the thief said this: "Don't you see God is here going through the same pain you are, and yet you think He doesn't get it?"

Christ's descent to the earth took away any excuse we could have to avoid trusting God. I recommend that you study the life of Christ in detail, starting with His death by crucifixion. I know that we all get the concept of His death, but we don't witness crucifixions very often, so we might be desensitized to what it really was like. Crucifixion is a painful, horrible way to die, and on top of being crucified, Jesus was tortured, ridiculed, betrayed, and abandoned by His friends. He felt hunger, fear, and pain, and He suffered the loss of loved ones. He was tempted, and He felt anger toward God and even felt abandoned by God. He had been declared guilty and was persecuted when He was innocent. He had gone through everything!

This is why understanding the purpose and life of Christ is so precious: it gets you so close to God. Do you feel that you have been unfairly punished? God gets it. Are you afraid of feeling pain? God gets it. Do you feel betrayed? God gets it! It doesn't matter what happens in your life. God tells you this: "I know how you feel. I have been there and done that, and I am here with you now. We are in this together, and I can see how this will turn into a blessing. I am here for you, so hold My hand, keep talking to Me, and hear My voice!"

I have gone through some hard times in my life, and I don't know what you are going through. I am very aware that your life may be more difficult than anything that I have ever faced. But I urge you to never stop talking with God, even if all you can do is share your sorrows with Him. Seek Him, and create the space for Him to heal you and give you strength.

I pray that this book will help you learn to hear God's voice and that it will encourage and inspire you to talk with Him about everything that you feel and everything that you do. I pray that you will talk to Him as if you were talking with a dear and close friend so that you may find your own intimate, personal relationship with God.

Marcos Borges is an attorney and theologian who lives in Seattle, Washington, with his wife. A native of Costa Rica, he and his wife lead medical relief missions to underserved people in Central and South America.

Made in the USA
Charleston, SC
20 June 2016